I Remember
Papa

The American Dream

Sylvia Elaine Liberati

authorHOUSE®

AuthorHouse™
1663 Liberty Drive
Bloomington, IN 47403
www.authorhouse.com
Phone: 1 (800) 839-8640

Published by AuthorHouse 10/03/2016

ISBN: 978-1-5246-2216-9 (sc)
ISBN: 978-1-5246-2215-2 (e)

Library of Congress Control Number: 2016912473

Print information available on the last page.

This book is printed on acid-free paper.

The views expressed in this work are solely those of the author and do not necessarily reflect the views of the publisher, and the publisher hereby disclaims any responsibility for them.

"I Remember Papa"

I. In the Beginning – In the Old World
   A. Italy – His Papa, Pietro Liberati
   B. Tagliacozzo – Ed's Visit
   C. Family Obligation – His Father's Death Wish

II. New World
   A. Hardships/Language/Climate/Family in Italy
   B. Positives in Pittsburgh/Good Prep/Jobs/Dates
   C. English Studies

III. Love/Marriage/Family/Deaths

IV. Perseverance
   A. Papa's Strength in Hard Times
   B. Eventual Successes

V. Family/Education
   A. Livia Teresa Liberati Gamboa –
      (Argenis, Gabriela, Roberto) – 1921
   B. Lola Isabel Liberati Tomassetti
      (Albert, Al Jr., Velma, Berard, Alexa) – 1924
   C. Edward Pierre Liberati – (Marceil) – 1927
   D. Velma Laura Liberati – (Deceased) – 1929
   E. Vera Elizabeth Liberati Deflin –
      (Ralph, Bradford, Marc) 1932
   F. Sylvia Elaine Liberati Rooney-Rosencrans –
      (Richard, Kevin, Darragh, Brian) – 1935

VI. Hobbies/Pastimes

VII. What's Not to Remember

INTRODUCTION

Ah, yes, I remember Papa, or Daddy, as we also called him sometimes. What memories!

I was partially inspired to write this book by the fact that my sister, Lola's, beloved husband, Al Tomassetti, would often refer to my Papa as "The Greatest Man That Ever Lived". And, I am in full agreement with Al!

Papa was, indeed, "The American Dream" personified…..

Yes, in The United States of America everything is possible with good hard work, the correct attitude and a lot of help from the good Lord!

Much of what you will read, in the pages that follow, will help you to understand why and how this man earned the love and respect of everyone who ever knew him.

Papa was always an example to be followed by those who have been so blessed as to grow up under his watchful (although, at the time, we might have said "strict") eye.

Come along now and "lend me your ears" and I will tell you the story of his and his family's lives, which, at times, will read like a fairy tale.

Albert Tomassetti Sr.

IN THE BEGINNING
- IN THE OLD WORLD

My Papa, Edoardo Liberati, was born in a small resort town just outside of and north of Rome, Italy, on December 6, 1891. The town called Tagliacozzo (which in Italian means little carved thing) is referred to in Dante's "Inferno - Verses 15-20":

"or where beyond 15
Thy walls, 0 Tagliacozzo, 1: without arms
The old Alardo conquer'd; and his limbs
One were to show transpierced, another his
Clean lopt away; a spectacle like this
Were but a thing of naught, to the hideous sight *20*
Of the ninth chasm."

As a young teen, he was called to his father, Pietro Liberati's bedside to be told of his father's imminent death, and that he would be responsible for the care and maintenance of his older sister, Agatha, and two younger brothers, Amore and Alessandro.

His father died in 1908, when Papa was just 17 years of age. Now my Papa would become the sole bread-winner of the family. He took this charge very seriously and attended trade-school to become a master machinist. However, in those early times in Italy there was little call for such a trade nor for a person with his expertise in the field. Needless to say, the responsibility weighed heavy on his shoulders.

One fine day, however, he was approached by his wealthy cousin, Theresa Colontoni, who made him an offer he could not refuse: "I will be travelling to Pittsburgh, Pennsylvania soon to join my husband. As you know, I am pregnant and already have young twins. If you agree to accompany me on the arduous, long trip across the Atlantic, I will pay your way. You can then work, make your "fortune" in the New World and return to Italy to take care of your family as requested by your father."

Papa did accompany his cousin to Pittsburgh but always had the intent to return to Italy. However, he met my mother, Amelia Strazza, fell in love, got married and they had six children, five girls and one boy.

Of that lot, I am the youngest who was only one and a half when she passed away. As a result of my very young year of age, I have no recollection of a mother. I did have a spectacular father, Edoardo Nicolas Liberati.

So please, lend me your ears (and eyes)!

Although he was never even able to finish high school, he had been blessed with a most brilliant and curious mind.

The following pages are several interesting stories about my father's birthplace, Provincia Aquila, the largest of the four provinces of Abruzzo.

ABRUZZO, ITALIA

The Province of L'Aquila is located in the heart of Abruzzo, and is surrounded by the Provinces of Teramo, Pescara and Chieti, Molise and Lazio.

The Province of L'Aquila is the largest of Abruzza's four provinces and is the only province without access to the sea. Abruzzo presents a great variety of customs and traditions as well as a diverse history. Because of this diversity, the people of Avezzano and Sulmona, situated in the Abruzzo region, have long expressed their wish for an independent provincehood. The territory of L'Aquila is this region's most mountainous and offers the most attractive landscapes, picturesque villages and natural beauty along its mountains and valleys.

The history of the L'Aquila is the history of this entire region. Its religious history dates back to the 15th Century, when the first Franciscan Saints appeared in the Province. The modern era did not damage the cities of Abruzzo until the earthquake of April 2009, when the L'Aquila Province was devastated. The Province continues to preserve its natural endowments, including the oldest park in Italy, the Abruzzo, Lazio and Molise National Park.

L'AQUILA –
EARTHQUAKE FAMILY TIES

When I heard of the devastation to the town of L'Aquila, Italia, as it came over the news recently, I was particularly upset, saddened, and concerned. My beloved father, Edoardo Liberati (1891-1985), was born in Provincia L'Aquila, in a town called Tagliacozzo ("Carved Thing"), approximately 25 miles from the town of L'Aquila, just a short trip outside of Rome to the beautiful resort hills of the area. Indeed, all of the surviving relatives on his side of the family still maintain vacation homes in the area. All of our Italian-American family has had the opportunity to visit this beautiful little town carved out of the mountain sides.

I was able to make immediate contact with our family in the area and they informed me that the damage in Tagliacozzo was not extensive, but that thousands in the area had been left homeless because of the severe damage to the homes, schools, churches, places of business, historical buildings, etc. Much needed aide has poured in from all over the world. Amen!

However, there was another reason why I was so touched by the news from L'Aquila: Right after World War II, I became the designated assistant to my father as we purchased, boxed and mailed our weekly "care package" of coffee, tea, powdered milk, dried beans, flour, sugar, shoes, clothing and anything else that was permitted to be mailed to our relatives in the war-ridden hills of Provincia L'Aquila. My particular expertise was in the wrapping and labeling of the package, after my father finished stuffing all he could into it. And I mean STUFFED! In fact, when my brother, Edward, Jr., visited Tagliacozzo while serving in the Army Air Corps after the war, he easily recognized my four cousins by their attire. It had been HIS ATTIRE before my father decided that he would "stuff" it all into the packages we sent to Italy to the less fortunate. How rich can a story be?

I do not know how many packages we sent, but I do know that we never missed a Saturday's mailing for years to come. Go figure! That's how many times I wrote "Provincia L'Aquila" on those packages!!!!

He never forgot his roots in Provincia L'Aquila, and neither can I. Get Well Soon Provincia L'Aquila.

NOTES FROM ITALY (Communicated in Spanish as we did not learn Italian but were fluent in Spanish, as were they in Italy).

Next Event
IAA Bocce Event – May 15 ... see p.2

Messaggio di Presidente

By now, we have already heard about the devastating **earthquake** that shook the L'Aquila area in the Abruzzo region of Italy. Although the story has, for the most part, faded from the front pages of the local newspapers and evening news reports, please know that the destruction and suffering left in the aftermath of the earthquake **are still very real**. With this image in mind, my message will be brief. In our attempt to help ease the pain of those in L'Aquila, Lou Perry, Vice President of the IAA, is leading the local efforts in organizing an earthquake relief benefit titled "Taste of Italy for L'Aquila". The event will take place on June 14, 2009 at Fred Grisanti Restaurant in Jeffersontown. I do not need to say much here about the fundraiser because you can find a more detailed description of it in the column to the right. You will also be receiving additional information in subsequent correspondence. However, what I would like to say now is Lou will need for all of the IAA members to contribute in any way that they can to this event. Such contributions might be in the form of **volunteering** at the event, **selling tickets** to the event, securing or donating **items** for the **silent and live auctions**, and **spreading the word** about the event to your family, friends, neighbors, and co-workers. All of our efforts are needed to help make this event a success because **100% of the proceeds** will go to those suffering in the L'Aquila area. So, call or email Lou and let him know what you can do to HELP raise money for the cause. If you would like to know more about how you can assist in the relief effort, or offer your specific expertise, please contact Lou Perry by phone at 502-231-7702 or e-mail at L4Perri@aol.com.

In addition to working with all of the IAA members on the relief benefit, I look forward to seeing all of you at the next IAA event, which will be the **IAA Bocce Night** at Norton Commons Bocce Court on Friday, May 15th. For more detail about this family friendly event, see the **Che Passa?** (What's Happening!) on p. 2; or call chair Walt Carpenter at (502) 412-2458.

Warmest regards,
Bernardo J. Carducci, President

DEVASTATION — L'AQUILA AREA

April 6 – Earthquakes rocked buildings and strong aftershocks rained debris on screaming residents and rescue crews, and sent waves of fear across Abruzzo and central Italy. The death toll from Italy's worst earthquake in three decades had climbed to 235, and at the time, many more were missing. The homeless where sheltered against the chilly nights in the mountains, some 20 tent cities sprouted in open spaces around L'Aquila and surrounding towns. Field kitchens, medical supplies and clowns with bubbles —— to entertain traumatized children —— were brought in. Officials estimated that 50,000 people had been left homeless by the quake......now, that number has been lowered to 17,000 because many moved in with friends or relatives. Some 10,000 to 15,000 buildings were either damaged or destroyed in the 26 cities, towns, and villages around L'Aquila, a picturesque city of 70,000. Assessments of the region's prized cultural treasures —— churches, monuments and other historical sites —— continues.

YOUR HELP IS NEEDED....

The Louisville Italian-American community is sponsoring a fund-raiser at the memorable venue – Ferd's (thanks to the generosity of the **Ferd Grisanti Family**). Mark your calendars and send for you tickets:

When: Sunday, June 14, 2009
Time: 1:00 pm to 4:00 pm
Where: Ferd Grisanti Restaurant
             10212 Taylorsville Rd.
             Jeffersontown, KY 40299

DONATION: $35/person; youth (12 & under) /$15
Check payable to: "NIAF/Abruzzo Relief Fund"
Food Items: antipasto, pasta/entrees, salads,
             bakeries, desserts, coffee/iced tea/soft drinks,
             and more. Note – "No Alcohol"
Food Vendors: Your taste buds will dance in the authentic Italian flavors, invigorating pasta sauces, and sweet, savory desserts from an array of local restaurants and caterers.
FOR TICKETS: send your check to, Lou Perry, 7809 Windgate Dr, Louisville, KY 40291.
SILENT-LIVE AUCTION: we are in need of gift certificates, filled-baskets, and even bigger ticket items, etc.

CAN'T ATTEND: Please HELP by sending your DONATION to Lou at the above address.
ADDITIONAL INFORMATION: call Lou Perry - 231-7709.

Che Passa!
(What's Happening)

Don't forget that **"you don't have to be Italian to live/eat/have fun like one"**, so please invite your family & friends to our events, as everyone will always be welcome

MARK IT DOWN:
May 15 - IAA BOCCE EVENT (see below)
June 6 - Special Olympics -- IAA Bocce reference
June 14 - Earthquake Relief fundraiser (Penne)
July - Winery Tour
August 8 - St. Joseph's Charity Picnic
September 4-5 - International WorldFest
October - Italian Heritage Month (send in your idea?)
November 15 - IAA Elections - Dinner (Ciffon's)
December - IAA Christmas Gathering (sent in your idea)

IAA BOCCE EVENT, May 15, Friday at 5:00 PM; at the **Norton Commons bocce court**. Activity chair Walt Carpenter, IAA members and the Norton Commons residents will combine to form teams to challenge one another at "center court" – a beautiful, double-wide bocce court. Others will be provided demonstrations to learn and develop their skills in the nearby grass area before taking center court. This festive event will also be served by IAA members and NCs residents -- Kristin & Justin Gilbert of **"Gelato Gilberto"** who will have their "gelato cart" and its gorgeous, artisan-made, Italian ice cream there. Also, Louie (Luigi, for the day) of NCs **"Karem's Grill & Pub"** has indicated that he will be grilling court-side. So, with a hamburger in one hand, a gelato in the other, you can kick your bocce ball down the court.
Location: off Brownsboro Road (at the Gene Snyder), take a left onto Chamberlain Lane then at the "circle intersection" take a right onto "Norton Commons Blvd". As you go up the hill you come to a fork-in-the-road ... pick it up and park – you're there.
Prizes: NCs resident/business - Dr. Tami Cassis, Dermatologist, has donated a few prizes for the outing

This fun-filled event will sure to please, be you a participant or a spectator ..... bring your lawn chairs.

MEMPHIS ITALIAN FESTIVAL
May 28-30, '09 ...... Marquette Park
Admission: $7 Thursday, $10 Friday/Saturday

On Stage
Thursday Night - The Venus Mission
Friday Night - The Box Tops
Saturday Night - Larry Raspberry & the Highsteppers
Starship starring Mickey Thomas

Free Parking/FedEx Shuttle Audubon Woods
Campus, Park&Perkins.

BIRTHDAYS
CUMPLEANNO FELICE !!

maggio
may

Azzara, Marie 5-14	Patton, Cindy 5-8
Carducci, Bernie 5-20	
Gilbert, Kristin 5-8	Gilbert, Justin 5-28
Tubeless Tire 5-11-'47	Spano, Diana 5/29
Questberg, Nancy 5-20	Vaccaro, Ange 5-2
Pinocchio 5-30	DelSignore, Dans 5/3
Flitt, James Vito 5/21	Flitt, Patricia 5/2

L'AQUILA -- EARTHQUAKE FAMILY TIES

When I heard of the devastation to the town of L'Aquila, Italia, as it came over the news recently, I was particularly upset, saddened, and concerned. My beloved father, Edoardo Liberati (1891-1985), was born in Provincia L'Aquila, in a town called Tagliacozzo ("Carved Thing"), approximately 25 miles from the town of L'Aquila, just a short trip outside of Rome to the beautiful resort hills of the area. Indeed, all of the surviving relatives on his side of the family still maintain vacation homes in the area. All of our Italian-American family has had the opportunity to visit this beautiful little town carved out of the mountain sides.

I was able to make immediate contact with our family in the area and they informed me that the damage in Tagliacozzo was not extensive, but that thousands in the area had been left homeless because of the severe damage to the homes, schools, churches, places of business, historical buildings, etc. Much needed aide has poured in from all over the world. Amen!

However, there was another reason why I was so touched by the news from L'Aquila: Right after World War II, I became the designated assistant to my father as we purchased, boxed and mailed our weekly "care package" of coffee, tea, powdered milk, dried beans, flour, sugar, shoes, clothing and anything else that was permitted to be mailed to our relatives in the war-ridden hills of Provincia L'Aquila. My particular expertise was in the wrapping and labeling of the package, after my father finished stuffing all he could into it. And I mean STUFFED!

In fact, when my brother, Edward, Jr., visited Tagliacozzo while serving in the Army Air Corps after the war, he easily recognized my four cousins by their attire. It had been **HIS ATTIRE** before my father decided that he would "stuff" it all into the packages we sent to Italy to the less fortunate. How rich can a story be?

I do not know how many packages we sent, but I do know that we never missed a Saturday's mailing for years to come. Go figure! That's how many times I wrote "Provincia L'Aquila" on those packages!!!!

He never forgot his roots in Provincia L'Aquila, and neither can I. Get Well Soon Provincia L'Aquila.

by Sylvia Liberati Rooney-Rosencrans

Youthful Papa, Tio Amore, Tio
Alessandro and the four Cousins

HIS FATHER'S DEATH WISH

As mentioned earlier, my grandfather (whom I never knew), Pietro Liberati, asked my Papa to care for and maintain his two younger brothers and one older sister. Although my dad never returned to Italy to live there, he took his father's dying words very seriously, and to his own dying day, sent food, clothing and money to his brothers Alessandro and Amore and his sister, Agatha.

Alessandro became a civil engineer and Amore, a professional, classical violinist. The two of them married two sisters and each had two sons.

When Amore died in World War II, Uncle Alessandro took care of his sister-in-law, Amore's wife and their two sons. All of this with a great deal of support, in many ways, from my Papa. With Papa's continuing financial backing, all four of the sons attended the Universities of Rome and Milan, and graduated.

When Papa took up residence in Pittsburgh, Pennsylvania, he was gainfully employed by United States Steel in their McKees Rocks, Pa. plant, Carnegie Illinois Steel.

There, he excelled and rose rapidly to a supervisory position.

In fact, at the age of 66, he had to show his supervisor his round-trip ticket to Italy to see his brother, in order to convince that gentleman that he was serious about retiring from his full-time employment. Obviously, they really did not want to see him go.

THE NEW WORLD BECKONS

Papa made the trip to America, in the winter of 1908, with his cousin, helping her along the way to take care of her twins and her, pregnant with her unborn child. The trip across was extremely long and arduous in those days, something akin to what was later called "steerage", although I believe that expression was dreamed up for emphasis on the difficult journey those poor immigrants endured.

He spoke no English, he had never experienced the cold Pittsburgh weather of winter's ice and snow, and had little resistance to the freezing cold. Nor did he have adequate clothing to withstand the freezing weather and winds of the hills of Pittsburgh. He had no family nor contacts. Consequently, he was very much alone most of the time; but his gregarious nature helped him to make friends easily in Pittsburgh, Pennsylvania, especially on Mt. Washington, where he took up residence and where I was born and raised.

Ah, yes, Western Pennsylvania has long been known as "The Melting Pot of the World". No one was a stranger nor a foreigner. They were all just seeking the American Dream: to work hard, live a "Godly", and family-oriented life while stretching out a helping hand to those who needed it (maybe worse than they did) but still minding their own business. Doesn't that sound like a success story? And it was! Those early immigrants thrived on every speck of the offerings of the new world and they surely complied with the demands of good citizenship and reception into their adopted country. A great lesson to be learned and practiced today.

Papa's great attitude, in times of extreme difficulty, came into play and he started to look for gainful employ. He started down at the State Employment Office. However, I remind you, he spoke no English. So, when the recruiter came out to receive a room full of "lookers", and he shouted "Master Machinist", my Papa did not understand. Although, he had received that title in the Old Country, it was useless if he could not apply for the job.

The man standing beside him, Stasho, was from Poland, and spoke no Italian, but pushed my Papa up front to apply for the position that the recruiter was shouting about. Needless to say, they became best friends!

Mind, my Papa spoke no English nor Polish, and Stasho spoke no Italian and very little English. Go figure! That's what Pittsburgh was made of!

My dad was very fortunate to have his Master Machinist's title and training, especially when it came to applying for and securing a job with U.S Steel, headquartered in Pittsburgh. The corporation snatched him up and started, early on, to groom him for bigger and better responsibilities as well as a bigger salary.

His first challenge in this capacity was to learn English… no easy task for an Italian speaking person, as the pronunciation and phonics are completely different and sometimes difficult to hear and reproduce verbally.

Nevertheless, he attended night school classes and became fluent but even after 77 years in the United States, he still spoke English with an Italian accent and wrote it phonetically. No one had trouble understanding him, however.

Meanwhile, he was introduced to and fell in love with my mother, Amelia Strazza. She would later become his wife. They wed and produced a great family of five girls and one boy: Livia Teresa (1921), Lola Isabel (1924), Edward Pierre (1927), Velma Laura (1929), Vera Elizabeth (1932) and yours truly, Sylvia Elaine (1935), the baby of the family.

Unfortunately, my Mama, after 14 years giving birth, developed uremia, a deadly kidney failure which caused her to retain fluids and finally take her life at 36 years of age. As a result of my early age, one and a half, I have absolutely no memory of a mother. (See family photo taken just before her death when she had blown up like a veritable balloon from the fluid retention.)

The Liberati Family

Back then, the medical profession did not have the extensive knowledge of, or cure for, this renal infection and disabling disorder; nor was dialysis, which cleanses the blood of impurities when the kidneys are unable to perform this function, yet to be heard of.

Needless to say, my Papa, was devastated and left alone to take care of and raise six children, ages 14, 12, 9, 7, 4, and 1 and a half (yours truly). A daunting legacy, to say the least.

As he had always done with the responsibility of his father's death wish to take care of his family in Italy, my Papa took this latest "fate" with equal or deeper commitment. Let's have a look and how he made it all work and come together.

One by one, I will try to relate to you just how dedicated, responsible and successful he became in all of his familiar and professional endeavors. Each one of the six of us felt like his favorite and indeed, each one of us, without a doubt, was!

When you understand that we all were college educated with higher degrees or the equivalent in specialized fields, took piano lessons, ballet and tap dancing, voice and any other thing which tickled our fancy, it becomes a story out of the movies or fiction.

We also all studied and speak (or spoke) several languages which we learned while living, working and taking courses overseas.

All of this done only through his constant encouragement to reach our highest potential in all walks of life. And to become citizens of the world.

His profession got plenty of special treatment and plenty of TLC as well. While employed by U.S. Steel (The Carnegie Illinois Steel Mill in McKees Rocks, Pa.) he endeavored to improve the systems of production, and the corporation in general, with myriad patents for greater efficiency.

THE NEW WORLD –
ARRIVING IN AMERICA

ELLIS ISLAND – AMERICA'S GATE
& PORTAL OF DREAMS

There are several interesting articles concerning this great port of entry into the early immigrants "New World". My Papa never spoke very much about his experience there, and I truly believe that he was so bewildered by it all that he did not want to re-live it.

Nonetheless, when Lee Iacocca renewed our interest in the Island with the founding of The Statue of Liberty-Ellis Island Foundation, Inc., each American Immigrant was invited to be registered on the Wall of Honor and to receive their Official Certificate of Registration therein.

Attached is a copy of My Papa's certificate, which he extremely proudly received from Iacocca himself. There were two articles published in the Wall Street Journal several years ago about the workings and marvels of the Ellis Island chapter of the American Immigrants' story.

ELLIS ISLAND
1892–1992

The Statue of Liberty–Ellis Island Foundation, Inc.

proudly presents this

Official Certificate of Registration

in

THE AMERICAN IMMIGRANT WALL OF HONOR

to officially certify that

Edward N. Liberati

came to the United States of America from

Italy

joining those courageous men and women who came to this country in search of personal freedom, economic opportunity and a future hope for their families.

Lee A. Iacocca
The Statue of Liberty–Ellis Island
Foundation, Inc.

LIBERTY
1886–1986

17

View of Pittsburgh, PA. from Mt. Washington

The Liberati Family

Sylvia, Livia, Edward, Papa, Lola, Vera

Lola, Papa, Livia, Sylvia, Edward, Vera

FAMILY/EDUCATION

LIVIA TERESA LIBERATI GAMBOA

My oldest sister Livia, was only 14 years of age when my Mama, passed away. However, she took on the responsibility of a fully-matured woman, helping my father with the housekeeping and upbringing of the remaining, younger four girls and one boy.

She was, however, nurtured and educated as very few young ladies of her vintage were in those days.

I clearly recall my Papa, driving her to private language classes with Professor Parisi of the University of Pittsburgh. It was a long trip across town from Mt. Washington to Oakland, where the Professor held private classes, after hours, in his home.

We would all patiently wait, in the car, for her to be finished with class to then take the return trip home. This was several times a week and she had private classes in three or four foreign languages.

Imagine it, after a day's work at the iron works mill, my dad would arrive home, prepare or help us to prepare dinner for the seven of us, clear that away and then drive across town for these classes.

Noble……..to say the least!

My Papa's cronies would criticize him saying: "Why would you bother to educate your girls when all they are going to do is get married?" Needless to say, his foresight paid off for all five of us!

In like manner, in his inimitable way, he would endeavor to make us all aware of the value of international language abilities to help fit into the world we were living in.

When you imagine that this was back before it was "fashionable" to be an international, you can understand why his thinking was so unique. He would take all of us to any and all international affairs open to the public at the University of Pittsburgh and the Carnegie Institute (now Carnegie Mellon University) of Technology.

Livia was offered a job with Westinghouse Electric Corporation as a bi-lingual translator/secretary. The powerful, international corporation had been contracted by the Mexican Government to teach and train the Mexican engineers and managers, whom they had sent to Pittsburgh to learn from the accomplished Westinghouse personnel and my sister Livia, was the appointed liaison between the Spanish and English speaking engineers to make sure everything was understood. At least, that was what Westinghouse had hoped for!

Well, she did such a fine job that when the contract was completed and the Mexican group, I.E.M. (Industria Electrica de Mejico) was returning to Mexico City, they invited her to go back with them and to continue working for them.

When she approached my Papa with their inviting idea, he was very quick to appreciate what a splendid offering it would be for her to not only attend the University of Mexico in Mexico City, but she had been invited also, by one of the ladies with whom she had been working in Pittsburgh, to live with her and her family there. It was just another great opportunity to learn about and enjoy the Mexican culture in that familiar environment.

She stayed and studied at the University while working for I.E.M. This continued for a couple of years and needless to say, when she returned to Pittsburgh, she spoke Spanish like a native, so to speak!

Livia then went on to work for the Chemistry Department at the University of Pittsburgh as a bi-lingual secretary/translator and continued to participate in all international events there.

As fate would have it, there she met her future husband, Argenis Gamboa, a doctoral candidate from Venezuela. Argenis Gamboa later became the President of SIDOR, a national iron and steel conglomerate. He had been sent to Pittsburgh to study and to work in the mills learning every detail about the industry. This he had accomplished "par excellence"!

After they married, they left to live and work in Venezuela and my nephew, Roberto and niece, Gabriela, were raised

there. They too are multi-lingual and Gabriela has the
following to say about their grandfather, my Papa, Edoardo
Liberati.

Iolanda, Leo

GABRIELA GAMBOA

Trying to find a wonderful or unique story about Pupup, or Pappap, or however it was spelled, is a difficult endeavor: a man who had the virtue of making every grandchild not only feel like his favorite, but as the only one, is a task, to say the least.

PupPup was both mythical and enormously human. I mean, our grandfather could grow two different fruits on one same tree,.....obviously he had magic powers. Yet he worked hard with his hands, and to this day our greatest inheritance in this family is our love of making things.

The best was going out to pick fruit and vegetables, and later watch him sip his wine. I just loved to watch him work, always busy and knowledgeable.

Among his other magical powers was turning a barren piece of rocky ledge in Venezuela into a vegetable and herb garden.

The years when he went to spend part of his winters with us in the tropics were the happiest times for our family. Issues in the very particular dynamic of the Gamboa Liberati's - (!!!) seemed to vanish and I always wished he would never leave. Respect, he commanded. Respect and things sort of flowed. Thanks to this!

Those times I would listen to him for hours, telling us some profound secret about life which sometimes went right over our heads, not only since they were deep, but because of his heavy accent, which is why he might be PupPup or PapPap, who knows?

I still have the letters he wrote me, in his small, tight handwriting, all of which are required to be read out loud since if you don't pronounce it like he used to, you might not have any idea what their content is. And even then....I remember when I sat all afternoon at the kitchen window, the winter Aunt Syl got married, waiting for the "bulls". I must have been five and he told me even though there was snow on the ground, the "bulls" would come and eat in his garden. They never showed and I was very sad.

Many years later, when my ears were better attuned to his heavy accent, he was telling one of the other little ones to sit and wait for the "burdies" to come and I finally understood. It was the "BURDS" not the "BULLS" that I should have been looking for.

But what I remember the most is the aroma. To walk into his house in Pittsburgh, was to be enveloped by deliciousness, and the desire to eat, play, laugh, cook.

For me, everything was luscious and smelled good, even the Parodi cigar he used to smoke. And I wanted to stay in there and enjoy it forever.

Harry Potter had not come into being but I guess it was like walking into the Weasley home....strange and comfortable at the same time.

Everything about my grandfather was life and smelled of it. It was wonderful when we made sauce 'cause then we might get some on a piece of bread, or help get the fresh tomatoes, and bite into a fresh one. Everything had a wonderful smell and an even better taste.

I loved when I was asked to go down to the basement and get something, hopefully my favorite: pickled beets....

He will always be a hero in my heart, a man who came here with nothing and built a life, who had a natural wisdom that is enviable. I often regret he never got to see my son, but more even, I regret my son did not have the benefit of having him to give him words of wisdom and kindness...

As a child who looked in wonder at a tree with apples on one side and pears on the other (or red apples and green apples??) my grandfather was the man who could do anything, things I have never seen anyone else do, for sure! But, as a teenager, I'm sure he saved my life just by asking me once when I was having a very bad day: tell me how it feels, and then held my hand.

LOLA ISABEL LIBERATI TOMASSETTI

My sister, Lola, was born in 1924 and when my Mama passed away in 1936, she was only 12 years of age. Yet, the older two girls were called upon to run the household, to the extent possible at their early age. Therefore, much of the load was on the shoulders of my Papa, Daddy Liberati.

Lola was very active in sports and soon became very proficient in ice skating. Of course, my Papa bought her a most beautiful ice skating outfit and she wore it proudly. She went on to be a star at the Olympia Park Ice Skating Rink in Mt. Washington and elsewhere.

When she graduated from South Hills High School she was invited to go to Dayton Ohio where her best friend, Barbara Massey's father, had accepted a transfer. When she approached my Papa with the proposal, he could not refuse, as he realized that she had always had a love for airplanes and flying. So he gave her his permission to move to Dayton with the Massey family with whom she would live while residing in Dayton.

There, in Dayton, Lola could attend the University of Dayton, while she worked at Wright Field as a secretary, and worked for and received her pilot's license.

In addition, she fell in love with a handsome air force lieutenant, Dion Hoy, whose twin brother, Trevor was also stationed there at Wright Field. Unfortunately, during a test flight with Colonel Thurlow, Dion and the Colonel were both killed.

Lola was so heart-broken that she opted to return to Pittsburgh and live at home again. My Papa was ever, as always, so comforting and gave her the courage to take an active role in the Civil Air Patrol of Pittsburgh. She was not flying anymore but was instrumental in promoting and working at many air shows at local airports.

Lola also worked a full-time job and took an active part in our own family life, which as you can imagine, was never with a dull moment.

Soon Lola met up with Albert Anthony Tomassetti, a high school friend. They hit it off while renewing their friendship and that friendship became a marriage, after a short courtship. Yours truly was 11 years of age while my sister, Vera, was 14. We both participated in their wedding as junior bridesmaids. See photo of this experience herein included.

Albert had recently returned from active duty in World War II, in the European Theater, having participated in every major battle of that theater. Unfortunately, he developed what the Veterans Administration Doctors diagnosed as tuberculosis. Albert was hospitalized and Lola came to live with us again. When he came home, he too moved into our family residence. The two of them were very positive additions to our lives in every respect.

They proceeded to produce Al, Jr., and Velma, both of whom were born and joined our family residence. Berard, their youngest son, came later on after they moved into their own home, next door to us

My Papa, presented Lola and Al the piece of property beside our home and, as Albert had grown up in a construction family, he built a fine residence for his own family and Berard, another son, was born.

Albert soon left the construction/bricklaying business and was hired by Louisville Cement Company in their Sales and Product Development Department. In fact, he was instrumental in developing a coloring process for brick mortar, which became a very unique, colorful and unusual approach to bricklaying and the use of mortar.

He was asked to join the home office Louisville, Kentucky and he accepted. And, guess what? Along came little Alexa, another beautiful addition to the thriving Tomassetti household.

It was a hard decision to make as he and his family had loved living in their new home next door to the Liberati household, where Papa or PupPup, as the grandchildren called him, tilled approximately two acres of gardens with fruit trees, which he pruned with several different kinds of apples and pears on the same tree, along with every imaginable kind of vegetable in his garden. He also had green houses and hot beds galore for starting plants from seeds and trees from cuttings and dwarfs of their larger cousins. Those hot beds were legend in the basement of our home all winter long.

All of the young people would call my Papa, PupPup. Berard's appreciation of his grandfather has given a keen, well-deserved, and well-prepared interest in his recently acquired farm in Pendleton County, Kentucky.

See photos and memorial contributions of the Tomassetti's to this tribute to "The Greatest Man That Ever Lived", my, Papa as described by Al Tomassetti, my beloved brother-in-law!

Lola and Al Tomassetti with Vera, Sylvia and Papa

Al Tomassetti Jr. Nancy, Catherine, Ben and Alan

NANCY TOMASSETTI (AL, TOMASSETTI, JR'S WIFE) SHARES HER LOVE

I married into the Tomassetti/Liberati family but only after being part of it for four years as Velma's friend. I traveled to Pittsburgh, PA for visits and was part of the gatherings in Louisville, KY.

Edward Liberati became my PupPup in 1966, when I joined a Girl Scout troop and met Velma, not having a grandfather growing up made him all the more special to me.

Velma loves the tale where PupPup tied cherries to a tree in the back so they could pick them. Al tells of the delivery of manure for the garden and working it into the holding pond, mixing it with water to get it ready for the garden. It must have been wonderful to have lived next door to your grandfather. The memories are sweeter for it.

I had a wonderful 1973 honeymoon trip with Al and about 20 of his relatives to Caracas, Venezuela. Aunt Livia had arranged for Al and I to have a separate bedroom, while everyone else was sharing spaces. The hitch was.....PupPup had his bed in the adjoining office room. He was already counting on great-grandbabies!

We were all going to Uncle Arch's brother's home for dinner one night. We all climbed into the cars and took off. Once we got there, PupPup was missing!!! He'd been left behind. The driver went back to get PupPup, who was waiting patiently at the Gamboa's home. PupPup said he knew someone would come. He loved the Uncle's yard with its mango and papaya trees. Fruit ready to pick.

We took Catherine, our first-born, to meet her great-grandfather in Pittsburgh when she was a year old. He could not keep his hands off of her. We sat on the metal glider on the back porch for hours.

The best time was the year of his 90th birthday party. He had three great-granddaughters to show off. He made sure everyone knew they were his great-granddaughters. Can you imagine how popped his buttons would have been if he had been around to see the 10 great grand-children together?

I have a favorite picture, one I've copied and shared. We are at Aunt Vera's sitting in the dining room at the table. The picture is just PupPup in front of the china cupboard. He is smiling, enjoying the conversation with his Parodi cigar in one hand and a juice glass of red wine in the other. He said he didn't drink water as it "rusted the pipes." He drank his home-made red wine and Four Roses whiskey instead.

PupPup passed on the legacy of wine making to Al Tomassetti, my husband, who in turned passed it on to his children and others. Now the next generation has the knowledge. PupPup lives on in the hearts of those who honor his teachings and memory. I believe my children hold his spirit and creativeness. Each of them has a loving and generous heart and are able to create with their hands or their minds.

I understand that he did not want Italian spoken in his home. He was an American and so would be his children. I regret Italian was not part of his grand-children's life, but he left us with a few special words, "Hut" and "Swit".

We cannot package our homemade Italian sausage, even if the recipe came down through the Tomassetti side, without using "hut" and "swit" to label the type of sausage inside. "Hut" is hot and "swit" is sweet, phonetically written, in his own English.

Much love,
Nancy Tomassetti (Al Tomassetti, Jr.'s wife)

VELMA LAURA TOMASSETTI'S MEMORIES OF HER GRANDFATHER

There are so many stories to tell that picking just a few is difficult. So I won't. Instead these are my everyday memories that have impacted me all my life.

Spending my young years living right next door to my PupPup gave me many day-to-day experiences that just pop into my brain at odd times....His smile, his laugh, the way he would curse in Italian so we wouldn't understand him, his intolerance for lazy people, his quick mind (I swear the man read anything he could get his hands on)....or like rocking with him on the glider on his back porch, or picking something from the garden and eating it right then or seeing him sitting in his recliner "reading" and watching the news in the evening, or going to Penn Ave. and buying his "Parodi's" (the rope-like cigars he loved to smoke.) Or like the time I fell going up his outside basement steps and cut my nose....I was sobbing and PupPup thought it was because my nose hurt...he was soothing me and said the hurt would go away....I told him I wasn't crying because it hurt but because I got blood on my new tangerine orange dress that my mom had made me. He started to laugh and said don't worry about that I'll buy you a new one and then all was well.

Another memory is when we'd come home from school with our report cards and he was more excited than we were when we got good grades. He paid $1 for each A...a lot of money then...and great incentive to do well. But more than the money, we were happy when we made him proud. I remember his telling someone (I was eaves dropping) "that the least of his grandchildren would be mayor of London"...a lot to live up to, but also something to strive for...a goal to make him proud.

I remember thinking one time that my Aunt Syl's name was really the "by-bee" (PupPup never lost his thick Italian accent) as that is always how he referred to her...I figured out she was the baby of the family and that's what she would always be to him!

As we got older it was all about what you were going to study in college, what you were going to major in, what did you want to do after school and when were we going to get married and give him "great grand-children". He was proud of all of our accomplishments but never more than when we gave him his great grand-daughters ...he had three, Vera Elizabeth Vaughan, Catherine Tiana Tomassetti and Laure Christine Vaughan, before he passed. He beamed just talking about them.

When I married John Vaughan, PupPup was overjoyed.... Two reasons...John was in the steel business and now he might get some great grandkids....my brother who had been married 5 years still hadn't done his job and produced any.

PupPup was, of course, at the wedding, and I'll never forget when John tossed my garter over his shoulder to the waiting "bachelors" seeing PupPup "snatch" my garter right from the air and grinning like he'd just won a million bucks.

Some of my best memories are of PupPup working in the garden or "piddling" in his work shop…he was always working on something. He never minded if we hung out with him. I garden today because of the joy he derived from his yard and garden….and now I share that joy with him. I often think he's watching me and saying "look at the size of that tomato!"

One of PupPup's joys was his fruit trees and as kids we loved picking apples, pears, peaches, grapes, figs, etc. that he grew. We all loved fruit and most especially his sweet cherries. I didn't know until I moved from Pittsburgh to Louisville that Bing cherries didn't grow on "pine" trees. Seems every summer PupPup would go to the fruit market and buy Bing cherries with stems. He'd bring them home and carefully hang them from a small pine tree so we could pick and eat them fresh from the tree.

I treasure all these (and more) little memories. But I think what I treasure most is his smile and his deep and unwavering love and pride for his family.

Velma, John, Elizabeth, Christine, Danielle Vaughan

Berard Tomassetti, Susan, Nickolas and Noelle

Alexa, Kurt, Tony, Bela Beilman

BERARD EDWARD TOMASSETTI'S TRIBUTE TO PUPPUP

Early in my life I thought I was lucky, living in the greatest country in the world and being a part of an incredibly loving, caring, traditional Italian family. How could I ask for anything more?

Then, as I lived life with all its vast experiences, I soon realized that luck had nothing to do with it at all. Of course, I was fortunate that my grandparents sought to make themselves better by immigrating to the United States. But it wasn't luck that brought them here. It was that they were driven by an incredible work ethic and the drive to pursue the dream of living in America.

While I wish I had had the opportunity to meet and spend time with each and every one of my grandparents, that was not possible.

However, I spent a tremendous amount of time with Grandpa Liberati, otherwise known as "PupPup".

And what a tremendous and rewarding time it was. Such an incredible man!

His passion for life, people and gardening were beyond anything I have ever experienced, then or now.

ALEXA TOMASSETTI'S MEMORIES OF HER PUPPUP

Lola and Albert's youngest, Alexa, just slightly younger than my oldest son, Kevin, offers the following memories about her grandfather, PupPup:

"I'm the youngest girl/woman on my mom's side, next to three older boy cousins, Kevin, Darragh and Brian Rooney. I am also the baby of four who are 14, 12 and 9 years older. So I was babied by them and a big family, and also was shown life ideally, and as having only the best.

I first remember, and grew up knowing, that I didn't have just a grandpa...I had my grandpa, PupPup. And I will always remember his calling me "da by-bee", which brings special memories of his expression and his big hug and kiss that came with it, except for the fact, which we all knew, that he called every baby in the family "da by-bee", beginning with his own baby, Sylvia, and following with all of his daughters' babies. Regardless, it was special!

I know that I, and believe we all might have felt his love in this and many other ways, and will forever be part of his memory."

EDWARD PIERRE LIBERATI

My brother, "Little Eddie", not to be confused with my Papa, "Big Eddie", was born in Pittsburgh in1927. Papa's dad was Pietro or Peter in Italian, and my brother Edward "Pierre" is Peter in French. Talk about an international background!

Eddie had a debilitating weakness growing up. He suffered from epileptic-like convulsions periodically which often happened at night. Consequently, my Papa would sleep with Eddie because this gave him a chance to be more vigilant of Eddie's need to have a tablespoon pressed on his tongue to prevent Eddie's swallowing it...........or at least that is what was believed and recommended in those early and teenage years of Eddie's life.

Doctors insisted that Eddie would outgrow the seizures in his late teens and he did, but it had weighed heavy on Papa's already heavy load that he had to bear, as you can well imagine.

Nonetheless, Eddie went through school successfully but quit when he was a junior in South Hills High School to enlist in the U.S. Army Air Force where he served faithfully. He went through basic training and became a radio operator, until the Victory in Europe was declared (V.E. Day) and was shipped to Germany.

From Germany he could easily travel to Italy and visit my Papa's family in Tagliacozzo.

When he arrived there, Eddie was shocked by the narrow streets built on the sides of the mountainous terrain of the area, and where all social activity took place in the Plaza, as pictured in the photographs shown here. He sat down on the park bench to observe the locals at their best........chatting and socializing.

Our four Cousins in Italy

Eddie Liberati with wife, Marceil

My Papa took it very seriously and assigned me, his "by-bee" (that's "baby" with an Italian accent), to be his regular helper in obtaining, packing and labeling the weekly box to his war-torn family in Tagliacozzo.

But let's go back to my brother, Eddie's, story. When he returned from his military service, he finished high school and went on to take courses in accounting and office management at Duquesne University in Pittsburgh.

After working at several interim locations, he found a job with the Credit Association of Western Pennsylvania and the rest is history. Fifty plus years later, he would retire from that to enjoy doing volunteer work at the local hospitals and church to which he belonged with his wife, Marceil. They both played active roles in such praise-worthy philanthropy.

VELMA LAURA LIBERATI

My sister, Velma, was born in 1929 and died just 12 years later.

It is indeed a very sad story to tell but at the same time, a very beautiful one.

Although many young people and children are referred to as "angels", Velma was invariably referred to as an "angel" and she fully deserved this reference.

When my older sisters, Livia and Lola worked and studied, Velma became the "housemother", not only cooking and cleaning at the age of 10 or 11 but also looking after Vera, age 7 and yours truly, age 4.

I remember reading the notes she would leave for my sisters when they returned home late after night classes. They would read like a note from one's caretaker: "I was a little tired, so I went to sleep but I wanted you to know that I left your supper on the stove or in the fridge, I washed your stockings and I pressed your outfits for tomorrow and left them hanging in the bedroom."

Velma was a talented musician. My Papa gave her piano lessons and how well I remember standing round the piano, as a family, singing, after dinner, while she accompanied us on the piano. To this day I know the words to almost all the "old favorites" that were popular while I was growing up in such a magnificent atmosphere.

She was so musically talented that her junior high school music teacher, Miss O'Donald, gave her private lessons on the cello and Velma became quite proficient on the cello and played in the school orchestra for several years to come.

Suddenly, when she was just 12 years of age, she began to have extreme back pain and would retain liquids. Her beautiful body swelled up to twice its size with this retention of bodily fluids and infection spreading through her body.

Back then they knew little about this kind of ailment and would tell my Papa that "these were signs of growing pains".

Soon, Velma was hospitalized for observation and further care and just one week later, my Papa was called to the hospital as she had taken a turn for the worse.

I remember it well. It was a Saturday evening, my older sisters had not returned from work and us younger ones were not allowed in the hospital where Velma was.

At bedtime we put ourselves to bed only to be awakened by the sound of my Papa's footsteps coming up to bed in the middle of the night.

Then he uttered the shocking and sad news about Velma's death.

Needless to say, we all cried ourselves to sleep for many a night to come.

R.I.P. Beautiful, wonderful, special beloved sister, Velma Laura!

Velma, Vera and Sylvia

VERA ELIZABETH LIBERATI DEFLIN

My sister, Velma, was the "angel"; my sister, Vera, was the "beauty". She was born in 1932 and, as you can see, from the early pictures of her, she was born with perfect features, hair and skin. Ergo, born a beauty!

From an early age, Vera was admired for the perfection of her God-given, good looks but she also had the heart and soul to go with it.

She and I, being the youngest children for whom my Papa was responsible, probably needed and got his utmost attention. We went to dancing school and danced with Vera Liebau's dance festivals called "kermises" at the exclusive Nixon Theater in Pittsburgh, at a very young age and, in the spring for many years to follow.

After graduating from South Hills High School, where she had been a cheerleader for several years, she went on to Bethany College, outside of Wheeling, West Virginia and continued her cheerleading role until she graduated.

After graduation she worked for Rust Engineering Company in Pittsburgh (old engineers never die, they just go to "Rust"!) and soon thereafter, rekindled the fire with a college classmate, Ralph Allen Deflin, a graduate C.P.A.

They married and Ralph was soon transferred with United States Steel to their subsidiary, Orinoco Mining Company, in the interior of Venezuela, to a small town named Puerto Ordaz.

Bradford Allen, the older of their two sons, was born in Centro Medico of Caracas, Venezuela.

While the younger son, Marc Edward Deflin was born in Pittsburgh, the year Mazerosky hit the winning home run to win the series for the Pirates.

Curious, but two sisters ended up in that small town. And, it sure helped them not to get lonely!

And some time later, I was hired by U.S. Steel in Pittsburgh to work in its Venezuelan subsidiary, Orinoco Mining Company in Ciudad Piar, the mining town which railed the iron ore to the port town of Puerto Ordaz. Three sisters in the interior of Venezuela where few knew we were related because we had three different last names: Gamboa, Deflin and Liberati. What are the odds of that happening?

Many years later, Ralph was transferred to Altos Hornos de Vizcaya in Spain near the French border. After several years there, they returned to Pittsburgh's U.S. Steel's headquarters and settled down to suburban living in Upper Saint-Clair.

Unfortunately, Vera developed breast cancer, was operated on for a radical removal of her left breast. She had the good fortune of going for more than ten years, which used to be considered "cured". However, in her eleventh year free of cancer she had to have the other breast removed and too soon thereafter passed away at the tender age of 44. What a loss!

Vera and Papa with Marc

Vera, Ralph, Brad, Marc Deflin

PHOTO NO. 33 – The Liberati Girls: Vera, Sylvia, Livia, Lola

The Liberati Girls, Vera Sylvia, Livia and Lola

BRAD DEFLIN

My memories of my PupPup are mostly sensory. Smells, tastes, and textures; so distinct and unique, they mostly power my recall today.

My grandfather was a man of the earth. He worked with his hands and smelled of good soil and sunshine. Fresh lettuce, corn, beets, olives, eggplant, garlic, tomatoes, and whatever else could be cajoled from the local land, all permeated his skin and formed the base for the smell I remember so well, even today. This masculine flower, combined with perhaps the smokey whiff of a Parodi cigar, a hint of berry from homemade wine, the malt of a good scotch, or the splash of aftershave on family-night, mixed to form the scent of an organic truth that was uniquely and eternally his own.

Every element of his work with the land was brought to the daily table. Fresh, canned, jarred, pressed, or fermented, nothing was wasted, and all of it tasted of the glory of God. Fresh pasta hung in the basement under the watchful eye of Mason jars from above and the wine-press from below. Tomato sauce relentlessly bubbled on the stove and fresh garlic was never far. Vibrant colors ruled the kitchen and table, shimmering and succulent even to the eye. To sit and "mangiare" with this man, to behold the fruit of his craft, and to indulge in the sumptuous gifts of his connection with the earth, was a delight that transcends all my experience since.

The tactile memories I have of my PupPup are indivisible from those of smell and taste. The scrape of his whiskers, while abrupt on my youthful skin, were well worth the embrace, kiss and words they held. In his hold you felt muscle and bone, framed almost boyishly, but ever so strong and straight. His hands, knobby from decades of hard work, held me strong, and always soon were to firmly press a $5 bill into mine. His skin, olive, alive, smooth and tan. And his hair silver silk, youthfully thick, full and parted, just as it had been in every picture I'd ever seen from his years well before mine.

These senses drive my recall, and while they still provide great joy and delight, it is the man my PupPup was, the love he held for God, family and country, and the way he lived his life, that captures and holds my heart the most. His honor, his goodness, and his LOVE are the gifts he leaves that influence our family most today. And it is with this love that I remember him as I pen these words, as it is I remember him every day of my life.

Brad Deflin

SYLVIA ELAINE LIBERATI ROONEY-ROSENCRANS

"THE BY-BEE"

(That's me, the "baby", with an Italian accent)

When my mother, Amelia Strazza Liberati, passed away at the age of 36, I was only one and a half years of age and have no recollection nor idea of what a mother ever was. However, my Papa was both mother and father to me….. correction to all five of us girls and my brother, Eddie.

My Papa made a pact with my mother's oldest sister, Aunt Maggie, who had lost her husband and was left with eleven children, seven boys and four girls. He promised to do all in his power, including financial help, and of course, plenty of food from his magnificent garden, if she would look after me Monday through Friday when he would drive from Mt. Washington to Homewood in Pittsburgh to pick me up for the weekend. Quite a long journey back then!

How I would cry when it was Sunday afternoon and I would have to leave my beloved family to stay with Aunt Maggie. Mind, I was doted over by her and all of her eleven children; they were much older than I.

I would sit on the curb in front of her house waiting to go home each Friday. Sometimes my male, older cousins would drive me home on their way to work with my Papa in the Carnegie Illinois Steel Mill in McKees Rocks, but I would have to sit on the front porch of the Liberati home on Mt. Washington for over an hour waiting for the first of my siblings to arrive to let me in and take care of me.

Obviously, as I was just a baby, I was the one who needed the most TLC and care. And, believe me, I got it from everyone that I can remember, especially my Papa.

As a young child, he realized that my vision was imperfect. It was diagnosed as a "lazy eye" and would wander back and forth from "wall-eyed" to "cross-eyed" as I became more fatigued and had little control over the muscles of my vision.

Finally, at the age of twelve, when a young girl is struggling to look her best, my Papa contacted the physician who wrote the books on the subject, Dr. Murray McCaslin, at the famous Eye & Ear Hospital of Pittsburgh. He was able to correct the "wandering" eye but unable to restore the vision in my right eye and I am what is known as "legally blind" in my right eye.

None of this cramped my style: I was able to excel in school as a straight "A" student, I have almost never had a headache and no one was the wiser about my visual deficiency. My teenage over-all appearance improved considerably.

I went on to graduate from South Hills High School in Pittsburgh with High Honors and from Allegheny College with Honors in Modern Languages. I spent my Junior Year at the Sorbonne, University of Paris, France.

All of the above helped to qualify me for the distinct honor of being chosen to represent Pennsylvania at the Brussels World's Fair in 1958. My Papa was prouder than a peacock when my photograph appeared on the front page of the ROTO Sunday magazine. And he surely was the one responsible for my success(es).

Sylvia at the Brussel's World Fair representing PA

Sylvia's wedding with Papa

Sylvia Presenting President & Mrs. Carter with
the Venezuelan-American Assn.'s Book

KEVIN ROONEY'S THOUGHTFUL ADDITION ABOUT HIS PUPPUP

I have been thinking of any memories or anecdotes to send you that would fall into the category of stuff that you don't already know. Yeah, we all know that PupPup tended a great garden, that he was an excellent cook and that he made great wine. You already know that - so I have to come up with more precise memories that you may not know about or recall.

One thing I remember, in 1974 or whenever it was that Al and Nancy got married, that whole crew came down to Caracas for Christmas. We were having Christmas dinner at Aunt Livia's house, and PupPup kept pouring me more wine. Dad had to tell him to stop serving me wine - evidently it appeared that I had "had enough"!

Another specific memory: Some years subsequent to that, like in 1978 or 79, PupPup came down to Caracas to visit by himself. We were in Qta. Cien Meses at the time, I remember he spent a few nights with us and then went and stayed with Aunt Lee (Aunt Livia – familiarly). Anyway, we all went down to Maiquetia to pick him up, and I remember contemplating how weird it must be for a man who could remember reading about the Wright Brothers' first flight to get on a Pan Am 747 and fly down to Venezuela to visit his family. Not that there is an anecdote in that per se, but I vividly remember thinking that.

One more specific memory: I remember once asking PupPup why fingernail trimming scissors were curved. His response to me: "Because they have to go around the corner!"

I will keep thinking, and will send you whatever else I can recall that is not the standard run of the mill stuff that everybody knows.

Love,
Kevin

Kevin, Darragh, Brian Rooney

Kevin, Brian, Darragh Rooney

HOBBIES & PASTIMES

My Papa, Edoardo Liberati, was never at a loss for something to occupy his mind as well as his body.

Probably the greater part of his life was spent in his beloved garden. His skills were so well honed in this area that he was able to supply our whole relationship, neighborhood and several charitable organizations with plenty of fresh produce and fruit from his garden for months at a time.

He even "domesticated" a female goat, called a doe or nanny, so that he could provide goat's milk to local hospitals which used it for those allergic to cow's milk. His life revolved around milking "Rosie", his pet goat, because she would "cry" if she did not get milked regularly and on time.

In addition, we at home had two freezers in the basement which were stocked enough during harvest time to feed our family all winter long with fresh, frozen, home-grown delights.

During the winter months he would plant anything he wished to grow in the garden in hot beds in the basement of our home. He would identify what was planted in each and write on the side of each one whether it was "hut" or "swit" (that's "hot" and "sweet" with an Italian accent and written in his own version of phonetic English).

Yes, gardening was his principle passion. However, he had many other interests.

Each fall he would go to the produce yards in Pittsburgh and purchase the best grapes available for his wine making exercise to produce four or five barrels of wine.

Oh, I almost forgot, this was after he had built the wine presses and obtained the barrels from the local alcohol distilleries for proper wine making.

But, face it, you have got to know what you are doing to be successful at all of the above and more. Therefore, he was an avid reader and would research and study any subject that might tickle his fancy until he understood it completely and could dominate the subject. This, of course, was done in his easy recliner after hours of working in the mill and later, in retirement, after his gardening, wine making and anything else he choose to pursue and produce.

He loved the opera and each Sunday, while supervising the rest of us in cooking and housekeeping, he would sing along with the operas as transmitted on the radio. He had a very nice singing voice.

My Papa was also an impeccable dresser and knew a good deal about fashion, design, color and materials of all varieties. Here again, he taught us the value of "dressing for success". We were schooled in what outfits were for sports and picnicking and which were suitable for church or which could be considered more formal attire for occasions which warranted same. He, himself, owned several silk suits from Italy and all the accessories to go with them. And he wore them all with pride.

He also made sure that we had the clothing to live up to his expectations ...perhaps not a lot of clothes but the correct things for whatever the occasion.

Oh yes, and my Papa had a knack for well-being. He actually personified the "golden mean", doing everything in moderation. Ergo, he was never sick a day in his life and could, therefore, attend to the six of us offspring who had all the childhood diseases, some more severely than others. He was a master of home diagnosis and treatment. You see, in those days, people did not depend on the world of doctors and drugs to cure their illnesses.

In keeping with his ongoing physical fitness of tilling the two and one half acres of ground we owned, by hand, he made a habit of climbing a 60 foot high rope on one of our elm trees in our yard. Yes, hand-over-hand, up he would climb and then, hand-over-hand, come back down.

One time when we had a family barbeque in our back yard, my sister, Livia's husband, Argenis (Archie, as we called him) mastered the ascent, hand-over-hand, but slid back down instead of descending with the hand-over-hand technique. Poor Archie had his hands torn bloody by the time he got back down to the ground. Still our hats were off to him as he was the only male relative who ever even made it to the top, hand-over-hand.

Yet there was another great pastime which my Papa enjoyed and which I have not mentioned: it was the art of ornamental iron. He had the advantage of a friend who owned a very prominent forging facility for ornamental iron.

As Papa was a Master Machinist and could repair and re-build any kind of machine or implement, he would spend Saturday's at his friend's establishment helping to maintain the equipment while enjoying the facility to hammer out his ornamental iron creations.

PAPA'S HOME COOKING

Spaghetti Sauce – (for one pound dried pasta)

2 tbsp. olive oil

1 cup chopped onion

1 clove minced garlic

1 lb. lean ground beef

½ lb. ground pork

1 (28 ounce) canned Italian tomatoes

1 (6 ounce) can tomato paste

½ cup white wine

½ cup chicken broth

1 tsp. salt

½ tsp. black pepper

½ tsp. black pepper

½ tsp.each dried oregano and basil

Grated parmesean cheese (as desired)

OSSO BUCO

2/3 lbs. veal 2/3 shank

½ cup beef broth

1 tsp. salt

¼ cup flour

2 tbsp. each butter and olive oil

1 cup chopped onion

2 cloves minced garlic

2/3 cup white wine

1 (14.5 oz.) can diced tomatoes

Preheat oven to 350

Brown meat, remove and add remaining ingredients to cook in skillet. Return meat to ovenproof skillet and back until meat is cooked but not falling off of the bone.

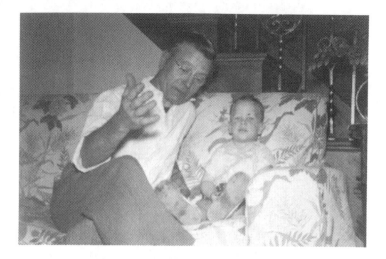

Papa and Al, Jr. with his hand-tooled
ornamental iron railing in the background.

In front of our home with his railing
and portico in the background.

MY PAPA – THE BENEFACTOR
AND THE DISCIPLINARIAN

You probably can imagine the gargantuan responsibility of not only having to guide and nurture the six of the Liberati children, alone, but also having taken very seriously the charge of his family in Italy, which responsibility his father, Pietro Liberati, had put on my Papa's shoulders when he was uttering his final wishes and soon thereafter passed away.

The Italy portion of that charge weighed very heavily on my Papa's mind throughout his life, especially when World War II allowed Hitler & Mussolini to take the whole country over. His younger brother, Amore, lost his life in the war. My Papa took the loss very painfully.

That left Amore's wife and two grown sons under the roof of his other younger brother, Alessandro, who was married to the sister of Amore's wife and who also had two grown sons.

During the War, it was impossible to send money, clothing or foodstuffs to Italy. However, once Italy was liberated, my Papa religiously sent funds, clothing and durable foodstuffs every week. And, I became his principal assistant every Saturday morning as we purchased, packed and "confiscated" any of my brother, Eddie's clothes and shoes. You see, as Eddie was serving in the U.S. Army Air Force in the European Theater, he would need new clothing when he returned home anyway!!!! At least, that's the way my Papa looked at it. (See my story about this in the article published in the Italian American Association's Newsletter of May, 2009).

I remember well how generous he would be when sending money to "the old country". In fact, his generous assistance put all four of my cousins through the University of Rome. How proud can I be?

And when it came to discipline, my Papa was once again a master. Although he never hit nor spanked us, he ruled us with an iron hand. That is, one stern look from him and each of us would fall right into line.

For instance, dinner time was a time for silence, until we finished eating. He would say: "When you are eating you are fighting with death!" He had experienced someone's choking to death while trying to converse and chew his food. And, if you ever knew just how many people choke to death in the USA alone, you would be overwhelmed.

However, after dinner we would all sit there at the dinner table and tell stories about school that day or whatever else we wished to talk about. He, in turn, was as great story teller and somewhat of a good actor. He loved to imitate Charley Chaplin. And then he would split his sides laughing about what he remembered seeing Charley do in the silent movie days.

OTHER FATHERS JUST LIKE MY PAPA

Several other fathers have been memorialized by their daughters in our local newspaper, "The Courier Journal", here in Louisville, Kentucky. Either could have been written by yours truly, as the messages all seem to parallel some of the things my Papa preached to my sisters, brother and myself frequently while he was single-handedly trying to make us into first class citizens.

I have included herein three of the most thought provoking articles.

The first, written very recently by Gail Lyttle, Vice President of Marketing for the Fifth Third Bank. Republished in Courier Journal.

The second was written and published some three years ago, in 1913. I have also included it for you to see just how much our fathers have meant to us. Republished in Courier Journal.

The third written by Doreen Snider and published in the Wall Street Journal

MY DAD TAUGHT ME TO BE PROUD OF WHO I AM

By Gail Lyttle

I grew up in Eastern Kentucky, the notorious, Clay County, no less. This, by the way, was a wonderful small town experience during the 50s & 60s, even though only a handful of black families lived there.

My Dad was a coal miner and my Mom, a home maker. I am the oldest of three girls, all of us strong, college-educated African American women.

On this Father's Day, I especially miss my Dad who passed away three years ago. I will always carry with me his faith, strength, sense of humor and pride in his heritage. He worked in Clay County coal mines for 25 years, until his lungs were so filled with coal dust that he could no longer endure. He did not quit working after mining, but instead moved on to construction labor in order to support his family.

The topic of my Appalachian background rarely comes up. Because of my parents' encouragement and expectations, I worked hard to lose the accent and earn a college education. Daddy always said "be proud of who you are, girls!". He lived by that and never, ever was ashamed of his country accent or any of his other unique ways, like interacting with people, for example.

He lived with me in Louisville for seven years and his actions, and others reactions, during every public outing took some getting used to. He always talked to folks like he had known them for years, attempting to start conversations with anyone and everyone he approached. Sometimes successful and sometimes not.

At first, I admit I was a little embarrassed. After all, we don't do this sort of thing here, and I am the spokesperson for Fifth Third Bank...what will people think? But this became interesting as I observed the reactions of people, in places, like the zoo, our neighborhood, his doctor's offices, the malls, or Wal-Mart, his favorite place to shop. Those who chose to interact with him genuinely seemed to enjoy it, and his conversation always came back to how proud he was of his three girls.

My dad was awesome! He was smart, though uneducated, and he made people feel good! I learned a lot during the seven years he lived with me...about him and his experiences growing up and raising a family in Manchester. Most important, I learned to embrace and be proud of my heritage, as an African American coal miner's daughter.

THE TOP 25 THINGS MY FATHER TAUGHT ME

By Elizabeth Schaaf

My father, Earl Schaaf, died Dec. 30, 2004, at the age of 91.

He was born on June 30, 1913, the only child of second-generation German immigrants who settles in Louisville's West End. He was struck by polio when he was 12 years old and lost the use of his left arm. He went on to play golf, build fish ponds and renovate his home. He also planted trees, drove all over Europe (at age 70) and has had a long and distinguished career as an engineer.

He and my mother married in 1938, had four children and celebrated their 65th wedding anniversary before my father's death. He lived simply and with reverence and respect for all people and the natural world around him.

Today, I honor all that my father taught me and celebrate what would have been his 100th birthday month. Following are the top 25 things I learned from him:

Life is a mystery. Don't try to figure it out; just enjoy it!

Oftentimes, the quietest person in a group is the most interesting.

Turn off the lights when you leave a room.

If you watch ants in a colony, you'll have answers to how humans can live cooperatively and peacefully.

It's easier to start a war than to end it.

Laughter cures almost anything.

Fancy houses and new cars don't make the man (or woman).

Be on time.

Practice moderation in all things.

It's possible for plaids and checks to look good together.

Don't buy on credit.

No good deed goes unpunished.

Tolerate differences in all people.

Reading history can help us avoid making the same mistakes.

Life is a circle: Just as space is curved, so is time. There is no beginning or end.

Always get a name when dealing with someone over the phone.

Lovable people are easy to love; it's the unlovable ones who need our love.

Never trust a turn signal.

It takes twice as long to do something wrong.

Ping Pong is a competitive sport.

Never litter.

Traveling is the best education.

Get along with your neighbors.

The Golden Rule is the only one you have to remember.

Leave the world better than you found it.

MY FATHERS CHRISTMAS LEGACY

By Doreen Snider

Around this time of year, when the temperature drops and decorations go up, I think of my father and the Christmas trees he sold to help support the family and to teach his children, and later grandchildren, valuable life lessons.

My father, Frank Williams, was a lawyer in our small town of Cuba, N.Y. He graduated from Cornell Law in 1936 and came home to start his practice. He met my mother and they were married in July of 1941. A few months later, after Pearl Harbor, he was drafted and served until 1946 in the Judge Advocate General's Corps.

Dad never complained about his service, but being away did put a large hole in his earnings. As a result, he and my mother decided to buy small tree lots for my brother, sister and me where we would grow and sell Christmas trees to use for our "college fund."

All of us would prune the original Scotch pines, and in later years we all planted first that did not require pruning each summer. The trees were sold "on the stump" to buyers from Buffalo. Dad loved everything about the business – the planting, the pruning, the anticipation. But he especially loved the days that the men came and cut the trees. He would leave his law office and go and count each tree on the lot, to see how many had been sold.

My dad even let us sell trees at the house. He thought it would provide good life lessons for children, and it did. We would cut about a dozen at a time, bring them home and put them on the front porch of our old Victorian house. We had a huge sign that read "Any tree $2." We strung up lights so that we could sell trees after dark, too.

What did we learn? Many things: the value of hard work, and caring for each customer, even those who couldn't afford to pay. We gave away several trees each year to people we knew could not afford one. My dad insisted on this, and never questioned or denied those in need.

My father died in 1998. That was the first year my family had a Christmas tree not chosen by him from his own farm. I cried while a man I didn't know cut down the tree I had chosen from a "cut your own" tree farm near our home.

I now enjoy picking a tree each year. The smell of pine and the sound of the saw bring back joyful memories. My husband I go early to have the best selection. Our son Paul graduated from the forestry school at Syracuse. He learned to love the woods during many hours spent with his grandpa on the three lot. Our son Mark became a lawyer. My dad would be so proud of them.

When our friends talk about how easy their artificial trees are to deal with, I smile. Christmas without a real tree is not Christmas.

Translation:

Dear Aunt Sylvia (Rebecca writes in Spanish)

Our grandfather Pietro resided in the USA between 1901 And 1907. He died in 1908.

Uncle Edward, your father, arrived in the USA at the age of 17, the year his father died, in 1908. He returned to Italy, for the first time in 1928 when his brothers, Amore y Alejandro were married. He came again to visit at the end of World War II.

Your brother, Edward visited here in 1945 after his service in Europe during WWII.

Ask me for more details of what you wish to have and, with the help of my grandfather, Pietro, I will answer you.

Kisses, Reby

My cousin, Pietro Liberati, R.I.P., gave me this great memory of my Papa:

It is with pride that I can help you with your book about Uncle Edy (the phonetic way Pietro spelled "Eddie"), especially since I am probably the only one who remembers a little about the Liberati Family along with what our Aunt Agatha (our great Uncle Edy's sister), born on December 24,1887.

"To begin with, their father, my grandfather, Pietro, had been in the United States and upon his return to Italy died in 1908."

Unfortunately, cousin Pietro also passed away before he could help me verbally with his memories and the love he felt for my father, who had remembered his father's death wish and sent sufficient funds to Italy to help educate his four nephews, two sons for each of his younger brothers, Alessandro and Amore.

Querida Tia Sylvia, (escribe Rebecca en Espanol)

Tu abuelo, Pietro, estuvo en USA entre 1901 and 1907. Murio aqui en el 1908. Tio Edoardo, su Papa, llego en USA a a edad de 17 anos,en 1908, despues de la muerte de su papa.

Regreso en Italia la primera vez cuando se casaron los hermanos Amore y Alejandro en el 1928 y la segunda vez despues de la segunda Guerra mundial. Tu hermano Edward estuvo aqui en el 1945 por unos dias.

Pidame mas detailles de lo que quieres y te contestare con el ayuda de mi abuelo, Pietro, su primo.

Besos Reby

PAPA'S CREDO – "I AM AN ITALIAN-AMERICAN"

I am an Italian-American. My roots are deep in an ancient soil, drenched by the Mediterranean sun, and watered by pure streams from snow capped mountains.

I am enriched by thousands of years of culture.

My hands are those of the mason, the artist, the man of the soil.

My thoughts have been recorded in the annals of Rome, the poetry of Virgil and the creations of Dante, and the philosophy of Benedetto Crose, I am an Italian-American, and From my ancient world, I first spanned the seas to the New World. I am Cristoforo Colombo.

I am Giovanni Caboto, known in American history as John Cabot, discoverer of the mainland of North America.

I am Amerigo Vespucci, who gave my name to the new World, America.

First to sail on the Great Lakes in 1679, founder of the territory that became the State of Illinois, colonizer of Louisiana and Arkansas, I am Enrico Tonti.

I am Filippo Mazzei, friend of Thomas Jefferson, and my thesis on the equality of man was written into the Bill of Rights.

I am William Paca, signer of the Declaration of Independence.

I am an Italian-American. I financed the Northwest Expedition of George Rogers Clark and accompanied him through the lands that would become Ohio, Indiana, Illinois, Wisconsin and Michigan. I am Colonel Francesco Vigo.

I mapped the Pacific from Mexico to Alaska and to the Philippines. I am Alessandro Malaspina.

I am Giacomo Beltrami, discoverer of the source of the Mississippi River in 1823.

I created the dome of the United States Capitol. They called me the Michelangelo of America. I am Constantino Brumidi.

In 1904, I founded in San Francisco the Bank of Italy, now known as the Bank of America, the largest financial institution in the world. I am A.P. Giannini.

I am Enrico Fermi, father of nuclear science in America.

First enlisted man to win the Medal of Honor in World War II, I am John Basilone of New Jersey.

I am an Italian-American. I am the million strong who served in America's armies and the tens of thousands whose names are enshrined in military cemeteries from Guadalcanal to the Rhine

I am the steel maker in Pittsburgh, the grower in the Imperial Valley of California, the textile designer in Manhattan, the movie maker in Hollywood, the homemaker and the breadwinner in 10,000 communities.

I am an American without sting or reservation, loving this land as only one who understands history, its agonies and its triumphs can love it and serve it.

I will not be told that my contribution is any less nor my rule not as worthy as that of any other American.

I will stand in support of this nation's freedom and promise against all foes.

My heritage has dedicated me to this nation.

I am proud of my full heritage, and I shall remain worthy of it.

I am an Italian-American.

ANDREA DORIA

July 25, 1956

It was 51 years ago at 11:10pm on a dark and foggy night, two great ocean liners, *T/N Andrea Doria* and *MV Stockholm*, collided near Nantucket, Massachusetts.

Andrea Doria - the most beautiful ship of the postwar era. Genoa, the home port of this ship, produced two of the world's greatest sea captains: Christopher Columbus and Andrea Doria. While Columbus went off in search of new sea routes and new worlds, Doria stayed home and fought off in turn the Spanish, the French and the Barbary pirates. Flying the flag of the Italian Line, the ship had a 637 foot long hull and reflected Italy's matchless heritage of beauty, art and design for 218 First Class, 320 Cabin Class, 703 Tourist Class passengers and 563 Officers and crew.

On January 14th, 1953 the *Andrea Doria* began he maiden voyage and was given one of Genoa's most heartfelt send-off..... every quay, breakwater and coastal road was thronged by cheering spectators and shipyard workers. The Atlantic crossing enjoyed fine weather, but conditions quickly deteriorated as *Andrea Doria* made her final approach to New York. Despite the storm, the *Andrea Doria* triumphantly steamed into the harbor.

In July 1956 the *Andrea Doria* was waiting for her 51st crossing to New York - a nine day trip. "La nave e in partenza!" (The ship is departing). After the spumante soaked buon voyage parties the whistle billowed against the red-white-green bands on her funnel, the blasts echoing against the hills of her home port of Genoa. First stop Cannes on the French Rivera; then on to the port of Naples, followed by Gibraltar. The voyage had been routine, yet the last full day out (Wednesday, July 25th) the liner coursed toward Nantucket and her rendezvous with New York the next morning, the midday sun grew hazy and the air humid ... the haze turned into fog. It enshrouds a ship like a dark blanket, robbing a navigator of his most treasured tool: vision. The *Andrea Doria* reached the Ambrose lightship, the last major checkpoint before New York Harbor. The *Stockholm* had left New York that morning and by nightfall had plotted a course that would take them approximately one mile south of the Nantucket Lightship. The *Stockholm* was off course from its intended route and the Danish sailor let his attention wander from strict observation of the compass needle.

The *Stockholm* was turning directly toward the *Andrea Doria*....... later, "She is coming against us!" The *Stockholm* sliced through the *Andrea Doria's* steel hull like a dagger stabbed into an eggshell. Finally, with the forward motion stopped, the *Stockholm's* engines, set in reverse, immediately pulled her back out to the sea, revealing a dark, open wound in the side of the *Andrea Doria*. The forward motion of the *Andrea Doria* continued to force the side of the ship against the broken bow of the *Stockholm*. The *Stockholm* bumped hard a few more times against the side of the *Andrea Doria*, shattering windows on the Promenade Deck and sending showers of sparks into the night. Those not immediately killed by the *Stockholm* prow drowned seconds later as the *Andrea Doria* heeled on her side never to rise again. The *Andrea Doria* was designed and constructed as a two compartment ship - theoretically "unsinkable". The once proud *Andrea Doria* is breathing its last!

ANDREA DORIA SANK AT 10:09 AM.

The lowest decks in the impact area became submerged immediately after the collision, and many of the casualties were members of immigrant families who boarded in Naples. On the Andrea Doria, 1660 people were rescued and 46 died. The speed with which rescue crafts arrived on the scene and the efficient manner in which rescue operations were placed under way saved the lives of many of the passengers, and crew of the *Andrea Doria*. Without such assistance the traumatic toll of life from the accident would have been much higher. The rescue work was conducted in the finest tradition of the maritime service. (thanks to Anthony Grillo, three year old survivor, and the Nautical Research Group, Inc).

After *Andrea Doria* sank, *Stockholm* sailed to New York City under its own power and was repaired. Later, it was sold to the East German government, who renamed the ship *Völkerfreundschaft*. She was transferred to a Panamanian company, who reduced her name to *Volker,* and later, she was Norway's barracks ship for asylum seekers. To make things really interesting the *"Stockholm"* was sold to Italian interests in 1989 and towed to Genoa, the *Andrea Doria's* home port. When it first arrived, the press called the *Stockholm* the "ship of death" (La nave della morte). It was refitted to be a modern cruise ship ... named the *Italia I*, then *Italia Prima;* she later sailed as *Valtur Prima* primarily to Cuba. Then she was acquired by Festival Cruise Line in 2002 and renamed *Caribe;* currently, the *Stockholm* sails as the *Athena* as a Caribbean cruise ship.

Sails - 09/12/2007; Caribbean; Cruise Name: Caribbean Winter Sunshine; Days - 32; Cost - £1999 to £2499

ANDREA DORIA FOLLOW-UP

by Sylvia Rooney-Rosencrans

I thought I would write some trivia concerning the Andrea Doria expose which you published in last month's (July) issue, and which I so enjoyed reading. One chapter, however, remains to be told.

I had just finished my junior year abroad in Paris and had traveled to Rome to visit my father's family in July, 1956. I tried, to no avail, to reserve passage on this magnificent ship for my return to the US. I had already reserved on the Ile de France, which sailed out of Le Havre France. Ergo, I had to return to Paris in order to board and head for home. Our trip was uneventful and we landed in New York on a Saturday night. The Ile de France re-supplied and was returning to France when the Andrea Doria was "hit" by the Stockholm. The "Ile" picked up some survivors on Tuesday and headed back to NY. I would have been on that Andrea Doria sailing had I been able to change my reservation from a departure from France to one departing from Italy. Wow!

But that is not the end of the story. After graduating from Allegheny College, 50 years ago, I was hired by KDKA-TV as Assistant to the Executive Producer. I was to replace Helen Castaldo, who was actually a passenger on the Andrea

Doria and was returning from her honeymoon in Italy when the terrible disaster took place. Needless to say, Helen had many a tale to tell.........floating in the Atlantic in a life vest and looking for her husband, etc. She and her husband were picked up by the Ile de France shortly after I had disembarked from its decks. Trust me, transatlantic crossings in those days were well worth it!

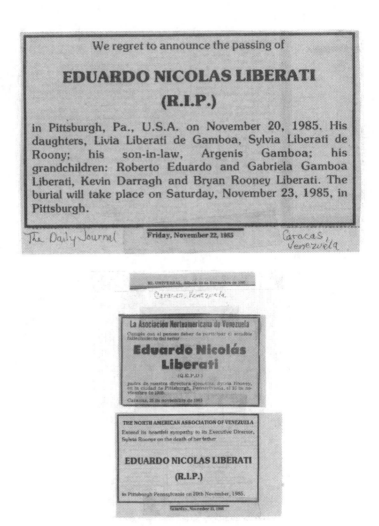

We regret to announce the passing of

EDUARDO NICOLAS LIBERATI

(R.I.P.)

in Pittsburgh, Pa., U.S.A. on November 20, 1985. His daughters, Livia Liberati de Gamboa, Sylvia Liberati de Roony; his son-in-law, Argenis Gamboa; his grandchildren: Roberto Eduardo and Gabriela Gamboa Liberati, Kevin Darragh and Bryan Rooney Liberati. The burial will take place on Saturday, November 23, 1985, in Pittsburgh.

The Daily Journal　　　Friday, November 22, 1985　　　*Caracas, Venezuela*

EL UNIVERSAL, Sábado 23 de Noviembre de 1985

Caracas, Venezuela

La Asociación Norteamericana de Venezuela

Cumple con el penoso deber de participar el sensible fallecimiento del señor

Eduardo Nicolás Liberati

(Q.E.P.D.)

padre de nuestra directora ejecutiva, Sylvia Rooney, en la ciudad de Pittsburgh, Pennsylvania, el 20 de noviembre de 1985.

Caracas, 23 de noviembre de 1985

THE NORTH AMERICAN ASSOCIATION OF VENEZUELA

Extend its heartfelt sympathy to its Executive Director, Sylvia Rooney on the death of her father

EDUARDO NICOLAS LIBERATI

(R.I.P.)

In Pittsburgh Pennsylvania on 20th November, 1985.

Saturday, November 23, 1985

94

Printed in the United States
By Bookmasters